Buildings

Nicola Edwards

A&C Black · London

You can sometimes see messages on the outsides of buildings.

This message tells you when the building was built.

The message on this building tells you about a person who once lived there.

Acknowledgements

Educational consultant Viv Edwards, Professor of Language in
Education, University of Reading.
Illustrations by Steve Cox.
Photographs by Zul Mukhida except for p. 2b Tim Garrod,
p. 3b Graham Horner, pp. 4,5t Kate Harwood, p. 7bl Tim
Garrod, p. 8t Tim Richardson, pp. 8b,9,10 John Heinrich, p. 11t
Tim Garrod, p. 11b Graham Horner, p. 12b Tim Garrod, p. 13r
Kate Harwood, pp. 14,16l Tim Richardson, p. 16r Tim Garrod,
p. 17 Tim Richardson, p. 18t Tim Garrod, p. 18b Oliver Cockell,
pp. 19,23l,23r Tim Garrod, Zul Colour Library, p. 3t Sally and
Richard Greenhill; p. 12t Paul Harmer, p. 13l Carlos Reyes,
Andes Press Agency, pp. 20,21 English Heritage.

The author and publisher would like to thank the staff and
pupils of Balfour Infant School, Brighton; Simon Hart.

A CIP catalogue record for this book is available
from the British Library.

ISBN 0-7136-4028-6

First published 1994 by A & C Black (Publishers) Ltd
35 Bedford Row, London WC1R 4JH

© 1994 A & C Black (Publishers) Ltd

Typeset in 15/21pt Univers Medium by
Rowland Phototypesetting Ltd, Bury St Edmunds, Suffolk.
Printed in Belgium by Proost International Book Production.

Sometimes people use buildings to write messages on.
These messages are called graffiti.

Sometimes people decorate buildings. What can you see in this mural?

Are there any messages on buildings in the area where you live?

There are messages inside buildings, too. They can help you to find your way around.

Which floor is the children's clothes department on?

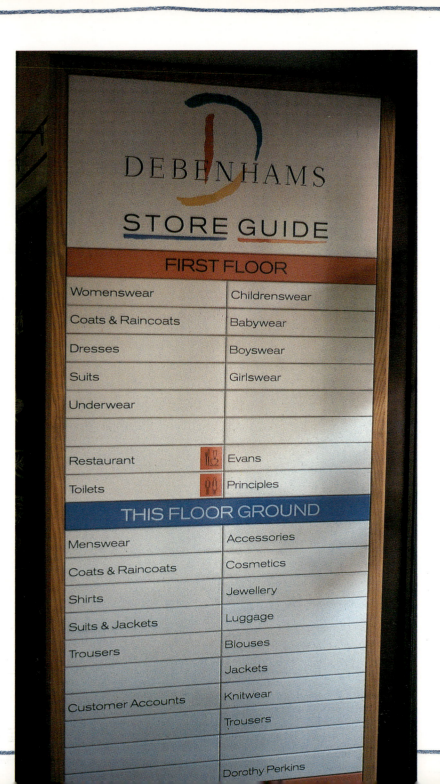

DEBENHAMS

STORE GUIDE

FIRST FLOOR

Womenswear	Childrenswear
Coats & Raincoats	Babywear
Dresses	Boyswear
Suits	Girlswear
Underwear	
Restaurant	Evans
Toilets	Principles

THIS FLOOR GROUND

Menswear	Accessories
Coats & Raincoats	Cosmetics
Shirts	Jewellery
Suits & Jackets	Luggage
Trousers	Blouses
	Jackets
Customer Accounts	Knitwear
	Trousers
	Dorothy Perkins

Which way would you go to find the toilet in this building?

Where would you be going if you went through these doors?

Are there any messages on the walls and doors of your school building?

You can also have messages about buildings.

An address is a message which tells you where a building is.

The addresses on these letters show the postman where to deliver them.

The address on this envelope tells you:

the name of
the house

Ocean House
25 Waterloo Street
Wickham Market
Suffolk
IP42 3PW
England

PAR AVION

the postcode
of the house

the town or
city it is in

which street it is in

**What other messages
can you see on this
envelope?**

**What's the address of
the house you live in?**

Some buildings have signs on them to show you what the building is for.

Look at the signs on these buildings. Which of them shows you:

Where you can catch a train?
Where you can have something to eat?
Where you can go for a swim?

Do any of the buildings in your area have signs on them?

Some parts of buildings
can show what they're
for without words
or signs.

What do you think this
building is used for?
How can you tell?

Why do you think the windows are an important part of a shop building?

What makes a lighthouse different to other buildings? Why does it need to be so tall?

Some buildings have lights outside them to show you what the building is for.

The blue light shows you that this building is a police station.

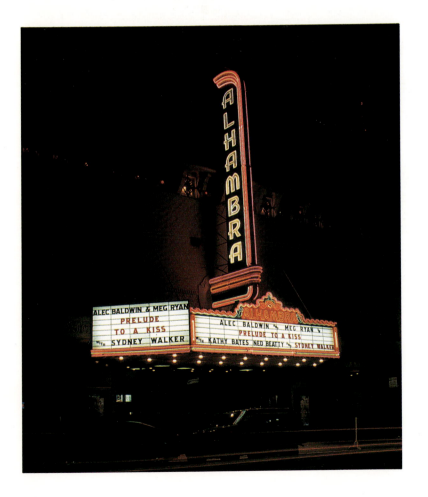

Lights can help you notice a building, especially when it is dark. What do the lights tell you about this building?

Some buildings use sounds to send out messages.

These people are ringing the bells in a church tower to celebrate a wedding.

The building in this picture has a security alarm. What do you think would happen if a burglar broke into the building?

Buildings where people live often
look different to other buildings.

Look at the building in this picture.
What clues can you find which tell you
that the building is someone's home?

Look carefully at this picture.
How many different buildings can
you see? What makes the homes
look different from the other buildings?

Here are three different buildings.
One is a modern building, another was
built one hundred years ago, and the
third was built five hundred years ago.

Can you tell which building is which?
What do you think the buildings are
made of? Which looks most like the
building that you live in?

Buildings can sometimes give you clues about the part of the world they are found in.

In New York City in the United States, many of the buildings are very tall and close together, because there is not much space to build on.

On the Greek island of Rhodes, many of the houses are painted white. This helps to keep them cool inside during the hot summer.

What clues do these buildings give
you about their surroundings?

Buildings can show when people are not looking after them.

What clues tell you that people haven't looked after this building?

This photograph of the same building was taken a few months after the photograph on page 20.

What differences can you see?
How can you tell that people are now taking good care of the building?

Throughout history, people have used
buildings to send messages to others.

When the wife of the emperor Shah Jahan
died, he built the Taj Mahal in memory of her.

What messages do you think the people who designed these buildings wanted to send to you?

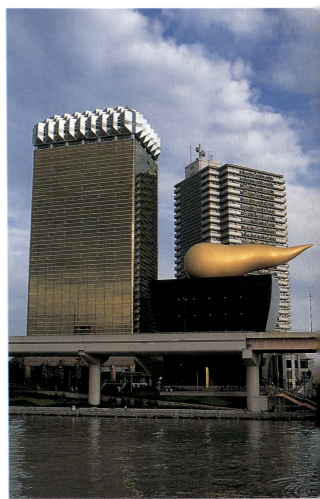

Index

For parents and teachers

The aim of the *Messages* series is to help build confidence in children who are just beginning to read by encouraging them to make meaning from the different kinds of signs and symbols which surround them in their everyday lives. Here are some suggestions for follow-up activities which extend the ideas introduced in the book.

Pages 2/3 Take the children on a short walk around the local area. Make a list of the different kinds of messages they notice on the buildings, such as, names, dates, plaques, religious symbols, signs, logos, graffiti, murals, clocks, flags and weather vanes. Back in the classroom, draw a simple map of the area covered on the walk and help the children to annotate it with pictures of the different messages they've seen.

Pages 4/5 Make a list of the messages that the children have noticed in and around school. The children could record their findings in a pictorial chart, grouping the messages according to those giving directions, those giving instructions and those giving information. They could also make up some helpful messages for the classroom.

Pages 6/7 Trace the journey of a letter from sender to recipient pointing out to the children the different messages involved in the process, for example, on stamps, in postcodes, on letter boxes, in the sorting office and on the doorstep signing for the receipt of a recorded or registered letter. Mark on a map, the distances travelled by letters written by the children to relatives and friends.

Pages 8/9 Using drawings or photographs, show the children a variety of signs on or outside buildings in the local area, for example, fast food restaurant logos, estate agents' 'for sale' boards, the notice outside a library and the advertisements for films outside a cinema. How many signs do the children recognise? The children could make up their own buildings and design their own sign or symbol to show what the building is for.

Pages 10/11 Make a collection of pictures showing distinctive buildings of various sizes, shapes and uses. Divide the children into pairs and ask one child in each pair to pick a card. The other child can then ask ten questions about the building, to find out, for example, how many windows it has, how big it is, what it is made of and whether it has a light at the top, before guessing what sort of building it is.

Pages 12/13 Make a collection of pictures to show how different buildings use sound and light to give messages, for example, door bells, security alarms, church bells, public address systems at football grounds, security lights and flood lights.

Pages 14/15 Take the children on a short walk in a residential area. Make a list of the ways in which people have personalised their homes. The children could make a model of a building in which they would like to live and decorate the outside to identify it as their home.

Pages 16/17 Collect some samples of building materials, for example, stone, wood, brick, glass and concrete, for the children to examine and describe. The children could find out which materials have been used to build the school or their homes and extend this by carrying out a survey of the buildings in their local area. Are the older buildings made of different building materials?

Pages 18/19 The illustrations on this page offer plenty of starting points for discussions about how the size, shape and number of buildings differ from place to place. You could show the children pictures of buildings in contrasting places and ask them to think about what each place might be like, for example, buildings built in different climates and contrasting geographical areas.

Pages 20/21 There may be a renovation programme in progress on a local building such as a church or block of flats which you could photograph at intervals to show the children how the work is advancing. What improvements do the children notice? What other improvements would they make to the building?

Pages 22/23 Make a collection, from magazines and travel brochures, of different styles of architecture. Which styles do the children like best? What do they think the interiors of the buildings might be like? What sort of people do they imagine live, or lived, there?